MW00640633

tell me somethin' good!

CLINT SWINDALL

For general information on our other products and services, please contact us at info@findthegoodinlife.com.

Swindall, Clint, 1967 –

Tell Me Somethin' Good: A simple guide to overcoming negativity/Clint Swindall

ISBN 978-1-7352771-0-3

First Edition: September 2020

Printed in the United States of America

findthegoodinlife.com

To Heather ...

my forever "somethin' good!"

CONTENTS

Introduction

We live in a negative world. We get it regularly from media outlets because it sells. There is no shortage of it from the people around us every day either. Coworkers, bosses, subordinates, friends, family, and strangers on the street will seek us out to share the crud in their lives.

Negativity isn't going away. We'll always have those who constantly complain about their situation. We'll always have those who are excessively pessimistic about their future. We'll always have those who simply cannot see past the challenges in their life.

While we can't eliminate negativity in our life, we can learn to overcome it. Since much of our negativity comes from old habits of dealing with the bad stuff in our lives, an effort must be made to establish new habits of dealing with the crud. When we do, we'll create a more positive life for ourselves and those around us.

For the past two decades, I have encouraged audience members around the world to find the good in their life and the lives of those around them. I've done it by using one simple phrase, *"Tell Me Somethin' Good!"* It's been fun to see how it has changed the way people interact.

I believe there is a significant opportunity for people to incorporate this simple phrase into a broader strategy to overcome negativity in their world. While part of the plan will be to build a culture of positivity in our own lives, it will include an effort to get those around us focused on their own good stuff.

In this quick read, I will provide a six-lesson guide. Each lesson will cover two behaviors. After you're done with the book, you'll have access to a 30-Day Challenge to encourage you to implement what you've learned.

This book is my third. The first two were business books published by a giant mainstream publisher. While I enjoyed writing them, this book is special for me. I've always wanted to write a book that could be consumed in one sitting. Not only do we live in a negative world, we live in a busy world.

While the size of this book is different from my first two, one thing remains the same --- it's told in a fable through the eyes of realistic but fictional characters. The brain likes a story, so I've chosen to use that format again because it works.

So, let's get started with our fable. The story is about Aaron King, an energetic call center manager wrestling with some recent personal challenges. In a world that surrounds him with negativity, Aaron faces an internal struggle to overcome his constant complaining and excessive pessimism from the current problems in his life. These troubles are impacting his personal and professional life. A long-time friend and colleague is about to introduce him to someone who will guide him back to the good in his life. Through a series of insightful conversations, Aaron learns a simple approach to overcome the negativity in his life. What may seem simple on the surface will prove challenging to implement.

The Fable

Aaron King was the kind of leader most people believed had it all together. He exuded confidence with his energy and desire to help others. His infectious smile and calming demeanor made him one of the most-liked managers at Halifax, a large call center company with offices all around the United States.

Aaron's calming disposition came from a seemingly composed life. He was a happy man. With a beautiful wife and three healthy children, his personal life was in order. With increased responsibility and success at work, his professional life was in order. Until it wasn't.

Even the most perfect life has challenges. Sometimes they happen a little at a time, and sometimes they all seem to come at once. For Aaron, they all came at once. His father recently passed away after a short battle with cancer, and his mother isn't handling it well at all. His oldest daughter is starting to plan for college, and he realizes he hasn't saved enough. Before these troubles, Aaron had not experienced multiple challenges all at once in his life. The new-found stress is impacting his relationship with Rachel, his wife of sixteen years.

Aside from the significant issues he's facing, the small things seem to be bothering him as well. Any time he turns on the television, other people's lousy news overwhelms him. Every little detail seems to be bigger than it is, from dirty dishes in the sink to lights left on in a room no one is using. Everything in his life feels discouraging, and he can't find a way to overcome the negativity. Although some people seem to enjoy wallowing around in their negativity, Aaron is not one of these people. He wants it to change. He needs it to change.

Aaron is hoping it all will change this week. After he gets his bag in the overhead bin and takes his seat on the plane, he thinks about how much he is looking forward to seeing his long-time friend and colleague, Seth Owen. If anyone can help him get out of this horrible place, he's certain Seth can get it done.

BACK TOGETHER AGAIN

The hour-long Uber ride from the airport to the hotel gave Aaron some time to reflect on the friendship he had developed with Seth over the years. The year they spent together in the Halifax call center was significant for their professional and personal development. It was a year he'll never forget. Both were fortunate to work for Hannah Jaxson, a rising star in the company who taught them more about being a leader in one year than most people learned in a career.

Although they live in different cities and no longer work in the same department, Seth and Aaron continue to communicate regularly. Each year they await the opportunity to meet face-to-face at a leadership conference in Newark. While they anticipate what they'll learn from the conference sessions, Seth and Aaron look forward to what they'll learn from each other --- and to the time they'll spend in their reunion with Hannah.

"You keep looking down at that cell phone, and you're going to get that thing they call Tech Neck," Seth laughed as he approached Aaron in the hotel lobby. "Not a good look, all hunched over like that!"

"It's about time you got here," Aaron smiled as he stood to greet his friend with a hug. "I've been killing time looking at all the perfect people living their perfect lives on social media. It's good to see you, my friend."

"It's good to see you, too," Seth replied with a smile as he sat down on the couch across from Aaron. "How was your flight?"

"It was okay," Aaron replied as he forced a smile. "I got a window seat and slept the whole way. It was nice to get some uninterrupted sleep."

Seth knew the struggles Aaron had been having recently, and he could sense his friend just wasn't the same. "I know you've been going through a tough time with your dad passing away. How are you holding up?"

"It's been hard," Aaron admitted. "Particularly for my mother. I'm trying to help her through it while dealing with all the other crud."

"Anything you want to talk about?"

"There's just a lot of stuff going on in my life right now, Seth," Aaron answered as he looked away. "Everything was going well, and then a string of things went bad. After my dad passed, I spent a lot of time trying to help my mom through the loss. In the middle of all that, my oldest daughter started talking about where she wants to go to college. I realized I am not where I need to be financially to send her where she wants to go. All this stress has caused me to become unusually negative, and Rachel has had about enough. She is the one person I need for support right now, and I'm managing to push her away. I guess even a wife can only take so much."

"I can see why you slept on the plane," Seth responded. "That much stress and anxiety can be exhausting."

"It is," Aaron replied as he turned back toward his friend. "That's why I've been looking forward to the next few days at this conference, reunited with you and Hannah to get recharged before I go back."

Seth paused for a moment before he shared the news. "The last thing I want to do is add to the list of bad stuff you just shared," Seth replied, "but Hannah called this morning and said she's sick and can't make it to the conference. This year will be the first we haven't had our reunion. It looks like you're stuck with me."

Aaron sat quietly for a moment. "You know, as much as that disappoints me, it's probably a good thing. I wouldn't want her to see me all pathetic, wallowing around in my misery. Besides, I came here hoping you might be able to lift me out of this crud. I've got to figure something out because it's starting to impact my personal and professional life."

"You'll get through this, Aaron. We all experience bad stuff. Sometimes it's small, and sometimes it's big. Sometimes it comes a little at a time, and sometimes it comes all at once. Regardless, we all get through it."

"I know that," Aaron assured him. "I experience crud all the time, just like everybody else. I just always seem to do a pretty good job of dealing with it. For some reason, I'm just wallowing around in it right now and need to share it with a friend."

They both sat quietly for a moment before Seth responded. "Sometimes, the best thing for us to have when going through tough times is a friend to lean on, and I'm certainly that friend for you. But maybe I can do more for you than being a sounding board and telling you everything will be all right."

"I'm all ears," Aaron replied.

"I have a colleague here at this leadership conference who specializes in overcoming negativity in the workplace," Seth said as he leaned forward on the couch. "Even though your struggles aren't in the workplace right now, maybe she can provide some thoughts that can help. She owes me a favor. Let me see if I can get her to spend some time with us this evening."

"I suppose that would work," Aaron half-heartedly agreed. "I'm not thrilled about the idea of sharing my baggage with somebody I don't know, but if she has something to say that will help me get out of this funk, I'm ready to hear it."

COCKTAILS

Seth enjoyed his year learning about leadership from Hannah. He found his true calling when he began traveling throughout the United States, teaching others at Halifax how to lead. Not only does he get to share his knowledge of what it takes to be a great leader, he also meets some incredible people who train on other topics. Michelle Chase was one of those people. She is a trainer who specializes in a problem Seth has long found intriguing, overcoming negativity in the workplace.

"Tell me somethin' good," Michelle said with a smile as she approached Seth in the bar.

"I'm getting to see one of my favorite trainers at Halifax," Seth replied as he stood from the table to greet his friend with a hug. "It's been way too long!"

Aaron stood quietly for a moment, hoping he wouldn't be challenged to tell her something good. "I'm Aaron," he blurted in an effort to lead the conversation.

"Hello," Michelle replied as she turned toward Aaron. "Seth told me all about you."

"Well, I hope we can still be friends," Aaron laughed as he extended his hand. "I bet you had no idea you'd return a favor by having to listen to one of his friends whine about his problems."

Michelle smiled and responded, "Any friend of Seth's is a friend of mine. Besides, I love talking about how we can overcome negativity to improve our lives. We'll have a great discussion."

"Well," Aaron laughed as he pulled out his chair and sat down, "if overcoming negativity is what you enjoy, then you must be one happy person. Everywhere I look, I see negativity, especially in our personal lives. Broken relationships, sickness, unhelpful people, unsolicited criticism, rude waiters, mean people --- the list goes on and on."

Seth chimed in. "It's not just in our personal lives. We see it in our professional lives, too. Disengaged co-workers, inconsiderate bosses, awful job assignments, corporate downsizing, racist remarks --- that list goes on and on, too."

"And there's a third list," Michelle added. "If we don't get enough at home or work, the media will always remind us of how bad everything is. Social injustice, divisive politics, dirt-bag child abusers, drunk drivers, high crime rates --- another list that goes on and on and on."

Aaron thought about it for a moment. "Look, I get it. With life comes bad stuff. If we live long enough, we'll receive news that will bring us to our knees. We'll experience hurt and anxiety that will require us to process life-altering changes. We'll witness friends and family that will face heart-wrenching mountains to climb. No matter how hard we try, we can't avoid the bad stuff. It's simply a part of life."

"That's right," Michelle replied, "and since we can't avoid it, we have to find a way to deal with it. There are different ways of processing bad stuff, depending on the severity of the news we've received. For instance, the way we handle losing a job will be significantly different from losing a parent. Life-changing events that stop us in our tracks require a very detailed and methodical approach recommended by some brilliant psychologists."

"I'm guessing you're not a psychologist," Aaron laughed.

"No, I'm not. I have a degree in positive psychology, but I'm not a psychologist. I can help people understand how positive human functioning can improve their lives. However, I can't help people with the difficult, life-altering psychological challenges in their lives."

Seth motioned for the waitress so they could order some cocktails before he added his thoughts. "Most of the bad stuff we encounter on a day-to-day basis is not life-altering. It's the crud of life ---a cashier was not kind at the grocery store, someone didn't invite us to a party, a 'friend' on social media made an inappropriate comment."

"Or a waitress takes too long to take a drink order," the waitress joked as she inserted herself into the conversation as she approached the table. They placed their order and resumed the conversation.

"You're right, Seth," Michelle continued. "Most of the bad stuff is just regular, everyday crud. And for our everyday challenges, we simply need a process. We need to wrap our heads around what just happened and put it in perspective compared to everything else in our life. We need to create a plan to get past the situation and lean on our friends for support. We need to make a note of what lessons we learned, and then we need to move on."

Seth smiled as he looked at Michelle. "If we lived in this perfect world where everyone responsibly processed the everyday crud, we'd all face the bad stuff head-on and deal with it."

"True. Sadly, we don't live in a perfect world. We live in a broken world filled with people who choose to wallow around in the bad stuff. These 'wallowers' seem frozen in a bad situation or bad news. They find comfort in sharing it with everyone they can find. They can't move on, and this is where it begins to impact others in the form of *negativity*."

Aaron slowly raised his hand and said, "I'm right here, you know. I've become the 'wallower' you're describing. I suppose I'm now in the group to blame for all this negativity."

"While it would be nice to blame the 'wallowers' for being the only source of negativity in the world," Michelle responded, "we are all to blame. You see, according to the

National Science Foundation, we each have up to 60,000 thoughts a day. Of these thoughts, 80 percent of them are negative."

Seth turned to Michelle and asked, "What?? We have up to 60,000 thoughts a day? And 80 percent of them are negative? That is insane."

"While that may seem insane, what's even more amazing is that 95 percent of our negative thoughts are the same thoughts as the day before. So, not only do we focus primarily on negative things, we make it worse by reliving the same sad, miserable stories over and over."

"Again, I'm right here, guys," Aaron laughed. "You are describing my life right now."

"I see people being negative all the time," Seth responded, shaking his head. "I had no idea we spend that much time focusing on all the negativity. Why do we do that?"

As the waitress returned with the drinks, Michelle continued. "Well, research shows we have what is known as a negativity bias. It's a tendency to pay more attention to negative experiences than neutral or positive experiences. Oddly, even when a negative experience is not significant, we still tend to focus on it over the neutral or positive experiences."

"Interesting concept," Aaron stated as he looked down at his phone when it buzzed. "Do you have an example of how we do that?"

"Sure. Little Johnny participates in a baseball game where he plays well. He gets feedback from both of his parents. His mother says, 'you did a great job,' and his father says, 'you've done better.' Based on the negativity bias, his father's comment will have a more significant impact on Little Johnny's psychological state and future behaviors than his mother's comment."

"I can see that," Seth nodded.

Michelle continued when Aaron looked back up from his phone. "The impact of the negativity bias is the same in adults. Here's another example. Karen gets a quarterly performance review from her boss and receives positive feedback throughout the entire review. At the very end, the boss was critical in one area of her performance. Based on the negativity bias, Karen is more likely to record that one criticism in her memory bank than she is to recall all the positives in her review. She is likely to categorize the entire experience as negative when it was very positive."

"I see that in my employee reviews all the time," Aaron added. "Someone takes one little criticism and blows it out of proportion."

"Any idea why we have this negativity bias?" Seth asked as he turned to Michelle.

"Some people believe we get it from our knuckle-dragging ancestors. Our ancestors had to work hard to survive. A simple trip out to gather food required a constant effort to deal with threats. To survive, they learned to identify potentially threatening conditions. Our ancestors constantly looked for the bad stuff. If they didn't, they likely didn't survive."

"I guess while they were looking *for* dinner, they were trying to avoid *being* dinner," Aaron laughed a little too hard at his humor.

"I suppose that is what they were doing. Survival required our ancestors to spend most of their time looking for the bad stuff. Evolution has assured that this self-preservation was passed along to us as negativity bias --- a technical definition assigned by some clever behavioral scientist."

Seth interjected before Michelle could continue. "I'm not sure I agree with that theory. I believe we get programmed from birth by the people we're around, and then we make bad choices throughout our lives that make us lean toward negativity."

"Fair enough," Michelle replied. "I'm not sure I agree with the whole evolution argument either. Regardless, the one thing I know for sure is they got the name wrong."

"What's wrong with the name?" Seth asked.

Michelle leaned forward. "They got the name wrong because there is a big difference between bad stuff and negativity. Bad stuff is what happens to us. Negativity is the constant complaining about the bad stuff. Bad stuff is what life gives us that is often out of our control. Negativity is the excessive pessimism about the bad stuff."

"Go on," Aaron responded as he slowly nodded agreement.

"If you lose your job, that is bad stuff. It doesn't become negativity until you complain about how bad losing your job was and how no one will ever hire you. Again, the lost job is not negativity. It's just a bad thing that has to be processed. If you have a mean boss, that is bad stuff. It doesn't become negativity until you complain to anyone who will listen about how horrible your boss is and how bad bosses always seem to find you. Again, the mean boss is not negativity. It's just a bad thing that has to be processed."

Aaron sat quietly and took it all in.

"Look, it comes down to one simple formula." Michelle pulled a pen from her bag, grabbed a napkin off the table, and wrote the formula:

$$BC + CC + EP = N$$

"This should be very interesting," Aaron laughed as he turned his phone over so he wouldn't see it light up when he received a text. "I'm guessing I know the first part. I've certainly had plenty of BS in my life lately."

"I'm sure you have had plenty of BS in your life lately, but it's probably not what you think. BS in this formula stands for bad stuff."

"You're right," Aaron laughed. "Not what I was thinking."

"What makes up the formula?" Seth asked as he leaned across the table to look at the napkin.

"Here's what it includes. When you add *bad stuff (BS)* to *constant complaining (CC)* and *excessive pessimism (EP)*, you get *negativity (N)*. As we discussed, bad stuff is going to happen to us all, and that bad stuff is not what makes us negative. It's the *constant complaining* and *excessive pessimism* that makes us negative."

Aaron sat for a moment and took that in before he responded. "That makes perfect sense. These past few months, I've had some pretty bad stuff happen to me. I normally just process it and move on. Recently, I have complained to anyone who would listen, and I've been pessimistic about things that have never even happened."

"I'm usually rather impatient with people who complain all the time," Seth added. "My typical response is to tell them to deal with it and move on. It seems some people process the bad stuff and lean into the positive things that life has to offer. In contrast, other people seem to thrive from their ability to live in the negativity. Why do you suppose that is, Michelle?"

"Perspective. Allow me to introduce you to two fictional characters with authentic scenarios. First, meet Brad. Brad experiences the loss of his job. He liked his job, so he's bummed. Brad's mind races through what it means as he wraps his head around it. He's got bills to pay, potential embarrassment when he tells his friends, and the stress of finding a new job. Brad puts it in perspective as he considers it's just a job. He puts together a plan to find another job and reaches out to some friends for help. As he's interviewing for a new job, Brad's making notes of what lessons he learned from this bad situation. At some point, he finds a new job. Brad moves on."

"I recognize Brad," Aaron responded. "I know a lot of people like Brad."

Michelle continued. "Now meet Andy. Andy experiences the loss of his job. He didn't like his job, yet he's still devastated. Like Brad, his mind races through the same things as potential unpaid bills, embarrassment, and stress from a job search. And for some reason, Andy finds more satisfaction in complaining about his situation. He complains that these things always happen to him. Andy says that if it weren't for bad luck, he wouldn't have any luck at all. Andy shares his misfortune with anyone who will listen to his pessimistic outlook. He whines that no one will want to hire someone his age, he'll probably lose his house, or the younger generation won't appreciate the value he brings to the table. Unlike Brad, Andy can't move on, and his negativity affects him and everyone around him."

"And I recognize Andy," Aaron reluctantly admitted as he realized it was a description of himself. "I know way too many people like Andy."

"Agreed," Seth chimed in as he put his phone down after quickly checking a text. "The same 'bad' thing happened in each example. One processed the lousy stuff and moved on, and the other wallowed around in it. I suppose the 'wallowers' create negativity when they can't process the regular crud of life."

"And we all know what happens when the 'wallowers' create negativity," Aaron conceded. "It starts to ruin personal and professional relationships, and when we allow it to follow us to work, it has a significant impact on corporate culture."

"That's exactly right. Negativity wouldn't be much of an issue if it only affected the person who chose to carry it. Those who can't process the bad stuff in life and allow it to become negativity because of their constant complaining and excessive pessimism cause it to spread like a virus. When it starts affecting personal and professional relationships, it's become a serious problem."

"I am living proof of that right now," Aaron admitted. "My constant complaining and excessive pessimism about the bad stuff in my life right now is bringing me down. It is causing worry, anger, stress, and sadness to my family, particularly my relationship with Rachel. At work, it is showing up as cynical thoughts, power struggles, denial, and bullying. Even worse, it's showing up as disengagement. We're always working to overcome disengagement, and I'm now contributing to it. My negativity isn't just impacting me. My negativity is bringing others down, and I'm breeding this culture of negativity at work and home."

Michelle smiled confidently. "That's what those psychologists like to call a 'breakthrough!'"

"Now that his eyes are open to the impact of his negativity, what does he do about it?" Seth asked.

"The good news is there are ways to overcome negativity, and I'm happy to share those. Before I do, we need to do two things. One, we need to take a look at two components of the formula: constant complaining and excessive pessimism. And two, we need to eat. Let's get out of this hotel and get some dinner."

DINNER

Any apprehension Aaron had about Michelle was gone now. He liked that she was sincere, approachable, and confident. These are qualities he saw in Hannah when they first met. It was clear to Aaron why Michelle and Seth had become friends.

As they approached the table, Michelle looked perplexed. "Mexican food? It seems like there might be some better places to eat in Newark."

"I'm sure there are," Seth responded as he pulled out his chair. "Coming to Casa Rio is a tradition for us. Back when Aaron and I first met, we worked for a lady named Hannah."

"I've heard you talk about her many times."

"Yep," Seth continued. "Awesome leader, teacher, and person. Anyway, the three of us would gather for margaritas after work back in the day at a place called La Cantina. We'd solve all the world's problems, or at least the ones in our little world. Every year we come to Newark, we come here as part of our reunion."

Aaron sat down. "Yeah, and Hannah got sick and couldn't make the trip this year. So, you get to be part of our tradition by having dinner at Casa Rio. I hope you like margaritas!"

The waiter came by and took an order for drinks and appetizers. Seth had him take a picture of the group so he could text it to Hannah. Since she couldn't be there in person, Seth hoped the image would lift her spirit.

Michelle picked up where she left off at the hotel. "So, I shared the formula with you --- BS+CC+EP=N. Let's start by taking a closer look at the *CC, constant complaining*. We like to complain. I don't know if it's true or not, but some research shows that most people complain once a minute during a typical conversation. It feels good. While it may not be good for you, it feels good."

"Speaking from recent experience," Aaron interrupted, "it feels amazing."

"To be clear," Michelle continued, "complaining is normal. It's not a bad thing. Complaining can be very beneficial when there is a belief the complaint will affect positive change. A complaint about poor service could result in better service next time. A complaint about lost luggage could result in an improved process for handling luggage. Constructive complaining is good --- constant complaining is not."

"Agreed," Seth responded. "We all complain. It's the people who complain all the time that wear us out. Why is it that some people are just chronic complainers, Michelle?"

"Well, research shows they've wired their brain to

make complaining a habit. You see, the brain wants to make things as simple as possible. For the most part, the human brain is lazy. It likes habits --- good or bad --- so it can create a circuit that will allow it to operate on autopilot. When the brain sees a repeated behavior like chewing your nails or eating a snack, neurons start communicating with each other. This communication between neurons allows them to form an alliance by connecting through synapses. This alliance wires a circuit to make it easier to repeat that behavior in the future. Essentially, the brain doesn't want to create a new path every time you think about something, so it looks for similar thoughts to trigger the same neurons."

"So, the brain creates habits because it's lazy," Seth observed. "Interesting."

"That's exactly what it does. This activity in the neural network is what a Canadian psychologist named Donald Hebb referred to as 'neurons which fire together, wire together.' Essentially, these neurons merge, and the connections become more long-lasting --- making it easier for your brain to know what to do with them."

Aaron thought about that for a second. "It sounds like repeated complaining rewires the brain to make future complaining more likely. At some point, we find it easier to be negative than to be positive. It's like complaining becomes our normal behavior."

"That's exactly right. And to make it worse, constant complaining is making people sick --- literally. According to a study conducted at Stanford University, complaining shrinks the hippocampus, an area of the brain that is critical to problem-solving and intelligent thought. Simply put, complaining makes you stupid!"

"That explains a lot," Aaron laughed.

Michelle continued. "And if that's not enough to encourage you to stop complaining, consider this. When you complain about something, your adrenaline gets going, and your body receives the message that it is time to get fired up to fight something. This message tells the body to release the stress hormone cortisol. The body can experience several negative effects of cortisol, including high blood pressure, anxiety, and sleeplessness."

"That may explain why I haven't been sleeping well lately," Aaron added.

"The more you complain, the more cortisol you have racing through your body. Research shows that high levels of cortisol can impair the immune system and increase the likelihood of high cholesterol, diabetes, heart disease, and obesity."

"Wow, that's a high price to pay for constant complaining," Seth responded, shaking his head.

They took a moment to place their dinner order before Michelle continued. "Now, let's take a look at the evil twin of *constant complaining (CC) --- excessive pessimism (EP)*, the last part of the negativity formula. Like complaining, not all pessimism is bad. There is a place for both optimism and pessimism in our life. We need a good balance between the two for our survival."

"I agree with that," Seth responded as he turned toward Michelle. "We all need some optimism in our life. We need to be hopeful and confident about the future. It allows us to see the good in things, which helps us fend off the negativity."

"I'm envisioning Wonder Woman using her magic bracelets to deflect negativity as it's coming her way," Aaron laughed, again a little too hard at his humor.

Michelle looked at Aaron with a blank face. "Yeah, something like that. Research shows optimistic people are healthier and live longer than their pessimistic counterparts. Their positive outlook allows them to see hardships as learning experiences. Perhaps most importantly, they are just more enjoyable to be around."

"I'm not sure I've been much fun to be around lately," Aaron admitted reluctantly.

"Likewise, we can learn a lot from those who are pessimistic. The Pessimistic Pats in our lives tend to see the worst and believe the worst in many aspects of life. Many lack the very hope and confidence we see in optimists. And perhaps most importantly, it is not nearly as enjoyable to be around pessimistic people."

"To which my wife would fully agree," Aaron replied as he looked down at the table.

"I'm guessing there is value to being pessimistic," Seth interjected. "We need pessimists to imagine the worst-case scenario in any situation, so we're prepared for it. I heard one time that people who worry a lot have higher job performance than those who worry from time-to-time. Pessimists help us by preparing for the bad stuff. At least that's been my experience."

"That is completely accurate," Michelle responded. "In the end, we need optimists and pessimists. What we don't need are the extreme versions of either in our lives. Eternal optimism is irresponsible and reckless, and excessive pessimism is defeatist. We need to be around people in the middle. We need to be around people who are capable of seeing the glass half-full *and* half-empty."

Aaron sat for a moment before sharing his thoughts. "Most of my life, I have been the 'glass is half-full' guy. Lately, I've become the 'glass is half-empty' guy, and I don't like it. I realize I will always have bad stuff in my life, but I want to get past this constant complaining and excessive pessimism. I'm not happy with it, nor is anyone around me. You said there are some ways to overcome negativity. What are they?"

"In time," Michelle laughed. "First, let's enjoy this dinner. We'll get to the details when we get back to the hotel."

For the next hour, Aaron had an opportunity to learn a little about Michelle. He learned she had her struggles raising two kids while traveling around the country as a trainer for Halifax. Aaron grew to like Michelle even more as he realized that someone with a degree in positive psychology encounters bouts with negativity. There just may be hope for Aaron.

THE FIRE PIT

After a quick break to check e-mail and return phone calls upon their return to the hotel, they met by a fire pit on the patio. Aaron took in the incredible view, then snapped several selfies before he sat down. "This view is amazing. I need a shot to put on social media later."

As they took a seat around the fire, Michelle commented, "I had meager expectations of your dinner choice. But I must say it was pretty good."

"Not the best food in the world, but the margaritas are good," Seth laughed.

"All right, Michelle," Aaron began as he got comfortable. "I'm ready to hear how you think I can get out of this funk."

"And I'm ready to share it. What I'm about to reveal to you are the six lessons I teach in my Overcoming Negativity in the Workplace seminar. Each lesson has two behaviors. I'll warn you now. On the surface, they may seem very simple. In practice, they can be quite difficult. So, don't let the simplicity of these six lessons cause you to discount them."

"Got it," Seth nodded.

"Also, to support the program, I have created a 30-

Day Challenge to encourage everyone to implement these simple ideas. I'll send you the link later tonight."

"Deal," Aaron agreed impatiently. "Let's go."

Stop Wallowing Around in the Crud

"The first lesson is this --- stop wallowing around in the crud. When bad stuff happens, we have this incredible power to determine how it will affect us. That power is called choice. While the bad things that happen in our life are often out of our control, the way we choose to react is completely in our control."

"Let me guess," Seth interrupted, "most people choose to wallow around in their crud."

"Exactly. We get to choose our reaction regardless of how overwhelmed we may feel when the bad stuff happens. We can choose to process the bad stuff in a healthy way and move on, or we can choose to curl up in the fetal position to get comfortable while we feel sorry for ourselves. Either way, it's our choice."

Aaron thought about that for a moment. "You know, most of my life, I have been the person who just dealt with my challenges. When something happened, I processed it and moved on. I guess I just realized I couldn't control the past. The only thing I could control was the future, and I always wanted to be an active participant in the plan to get moving. I guess I was making that choice."

"That's exactly what you were doing, and you had complete control of it. We also know some people who jump from one life challenge to the next wallowing around in the crud. Some people are so bitter and jaded about life that every bump in the road becomes a mountain for them to climb. They believe life has provided a black cloud to follow them wherever they go. They, too, have made a choice."

Aaron let that sink in. "You just described me the past few months. I felt like the negativity had control of me, when in reality, I was choosing to let it control me. Life is too short to continue making that choice. How do we stop wallowing around in the crud?"

"Two things I suggest you do." Michelle pulled out her notebook and a pad of those small sticky notes. "I would normally be doing this on a flipchart in a training room, but since we don't have one out here, I'll do it on this sheet of paper."

Michelle wrote on the first sticky note, peeled it off, and stuck it to the sheet in the notebook:

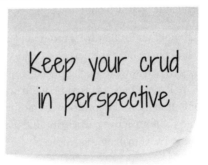

Keep your crud in perspective

She held it up for Seth and Aaron to read. They leaned forward and squinted to see what she had written. "It's going to be hard for you to see these sticky notes out here by the fire because they're so small, so I'll send you a PDF with all these notes along with the link to the 30-Day Challenge after we get done."

"Awesome," Aaron nodded as he leaned back in his chair.

"The first thing you need to do is keep your crud in perspective. Keep in mind that regardless of how bad things are in your life, someone has it worse. If you're struggling with finance, keep in mind that research shows more than 50 percent of the world's population lives on less than $2 a day. If you lost a loved one, keep in mind that some people have lost their entire families due to a tragedy."

"That's true," Aaron responded to Michelle, "but it can sure be hard to think about other people's crud when you're standing in your own."

"That's why I said from the beginning that these things might seem simple on the surface but difficult to implement. Don't let the simplicity of keeping your crud in perspective allow you to push it to the side. There is something very powerful about perspective."

Seth considered that thought. "We all have challenges in our life that deserve our attention. Although the big stuff is really hard to get past, I suppose the majority of what we occupy our time with would seem insignificant if we kept it all in perspective."

Michelle paused for a moment to let it all sink in and then said, "Here's the second thing you need to do." She grabbed the pad of sticky notes, wrote on it, peeled it off, and added it to the sheet in the notebook:

Give yourself a time limit to immerse yourself in the crud

"The second thing you need to do is give yourself a time limit to immerse yourself in the crud. Look, the pain that comes with the bad stuff in life is real. Whether it's the loss of a loved one, the loss of a job, or the loss of your temper because the waiter got your order wrong, it's important to know it is okay to feel bad. It is okay to feel upset. It is okay to curl up in the fetal position to mourn the big losses. These are completely normal human emotions. To bury these emotions can have a long-term impact on your life when they come back to the surface. Some people get through them quickly, and others take longer. Either way, take the time to deal with those emotions."

"I've been taking time to process the loss of my dad," Aaron quietly responded. "At some point, I feel I went from processing my emotions to wallowing around in them and feeling sorry for myself."

"That's very common, Aaron. To ensure you don't wallow around in the crud for too long, give yourself a time limit. The bigger the challenge, the longer your time limit. If you're having a lousy day and think nothing will ever get better, give yourself a couple of hours. Tell yourself that for two hours, you can be miserable, and at the end of that window of time, it's over --- time to pick yourself up and deal with it. Maybe it's a couple of hours. Maybe it's a couple of days. Maybe it's a couple of weeks for the really hard challenges. Whatever it is, give yourself proper time, then put together a plan to help you move on. You owe it to yourself."

"Life isn't perfect, for sure," Seth added. "We all have 'those' days, and when we do, we need to make good choices. While the decision to move on from the bad stuff can be hard, choosing to wallow around in it can have long-lasting effects on our personal and professional lives. When we stay too long in the crud, we harm ourselves and those around us."

They sat quietly for a moment before Seth continued. "What's next?"

Initiate Relationships with Positive People

"The second lesson is this --- initiate relationships with positive people. One of the most important decisions we make in life is who we choose to be around. An old proverb reads, 'Show me your friends and I'll tell you who you are.' Quite often, we become like the people we're around. Based on that, we have to be cautious about who we surround ourselves with every day."

"No argument with that," Seth replied. "We become like the people we're around."

"Yep, more than you may realize," Michelle replied. "Those around us have a profound impact on us because we subconsciously tend to mimic the gestures of people we like. This common human behavior is known as neuron mirroring. It explains why we become sad when we're around someone grieving, happy when we're around someone celebrating, and bitter when we're around someone complaining."

"I can see that," Aaron replied as he glanced down at his phone.

Michelle continued. "Mirroring can be great in relationships because it allows us to connect with and share emotions with those who matter in our lives. It can also be quite detrimental when we subconsciously mimic the negativity of those around us. Based on the potential negative impact of mirroring the bad behavior of those around us, we must initiate relationships with positive people."

"That's why I make an effort never to lose contact with Seth," Aaron replied, nodding toward Seth. "He's a positive influence in my life, and I can't say that about everyone around me."

"We all need people like that around us. Here's what I would encourage you to do. Take some time to analyze the people you are around the most – both personally and professionally. Are they excited when you share your successes? Are they supportive when you share your challenges? Can you depend on them when you need someone? Do they add to your life or take away from it? Are they a source of encouragement when you're down, or do they mirror your negativity in tough times and pull you down further?"

"That will be an interesting exercise because I know I have both types around me," Aaron acknowledged.

Michelle continued. "Once you've done that, there are two things I suggest you do." She grabbed the pad of sticky notes, wrote on it, peeled it off, and added it to the sheet in the notebook:

Filter out the
unreasonably
negative people
in your life

"The first thing you need to do to initiate relationships with positive people is to filter out the unreasonably negative people in your life. We have a responsibility to guard ourselves against constant complaining and excessive pessimism. When we don't, we allow the complainers to pull us into their pity parties to feel better about themselves. Remember, they are looking for someone who will mirror their negativity, and once you've joined their group, you've become one of them."

"Sounds like something we've learned from Hannah before," Seth remarked as he looked over at Aaron. "She's always talked about getting rid of the negative people in our lives."

"It's important to note that we can't just start kicking people out of our life because they're negative. If you notice, I said 'unreasonably' negative. In some cases, you may decide to remove someone from your life altogether. In most cases, you can simply limit the exposure some people are allowed in your life."

"Yeah, if I eliminated everyone in my life who expressed negativity, I wouldn't have anyone around," Aaron laughed. "That would be absurd. Some have been my friends for a long time. Some have worked beside me for years."

Michelle continued. "The good news is you won't need to eliminate most people in your life because most people don't fall in the 'unreasonably negative' category. However, you do have the control to determine whose access you should limit based on how they negatively impact your life. Limit those people and make some new friends. Find people who will be happy for you. Find people who will clap when you win. Find people who you can do the same for in return. There are nearly 8 billion people on the planet. Surely you can find a few who you can consider real friends."

"Fair enough," Seth replied. "What's the second thing?"

Michelle grabbed the pad of small sticky notes, wrote on it, peeled it off, and added it to the sheet in the notebook:

> Dedicate time to the exceptionally positive people in your life

"The next thing you need to do is dedicate time to the exceptionally positive people in your life. Go back to the analysis you did of the people around you. Now that you've identified those who are unreasonably negative, identify those who are exceptionally positive and dedicate time to be around them. These are the people who encourage you and lift you so you should commit time to them. Our lives are so busy that sometimes we have to dedicate the time to interact with the people who have the greatest positive impact."

"I guess I never think about spending time with people as a strategy in my life," Seth pondered out loud. "I just hang out with my regular crowd of people --- at work and in my personal life."

"That's how we all do it. Sometimes negative people show up in our life because we're supposed to help them through something. We need to fulfill that responsibility because it lifts them. At the same time, we need to be intentional about being around people who lift us. If you need to schedule time to keep in touch with friends and family who do that for you, put it on a calendar. Sometimes we have to make hard choices about what to eliminate to dedicate time to the relationships."

"I guess it's like that old saying that if we're around someone with a cold, there's a good chance we'll catch a cold," Aaron replied. "While it's important to consider what we're catching from the people around us, I suppose we need to consider what people are catching from us. The people around me lately haven't been catching anything good. My whole life I've been the one most people would consider 'exceptionally positive,' and I need to get back there."

"Well said, Aaron," Seth responded. "What's next?"

Manage Your Information Flow

"The third lesson is this --- manage your information flow. The amount of information we consume daily is enormous. The digital devices we carry are constantly buzzing, dinging, blinking, beeping, or ringing to get our attention. Information is flooding in faster than we can read it, watch it, or listen to it. We're drowning in information."

"Isn't that the truth," Aaron replied as he looked down at his phone. "I seem to always be on my phone. My screen time seems to go up each week."

Michelle continued. "Information overload is easy to understand when you consider that content creation is higher than it's ever been. Technology has made it possible for anyone with a cell phone and an idea to share it with the world. If you need to build something, fix something, clean something, or grow something, you can figure out how to do it within minutes. Without question, valuable content is making us smarter, but it's eating up our time."

"The problem is this stupid smartphone," Seth replied as he pulled it out of his pocket. "Between this and all my other devices, technology allows me to access that information whenever I want. I seldom disconnect from these devices. For me, technology starts the day. This phone wakes me up with an alarm, then immediately provides the e-mail that came in overnight. An app tells me what to expect with the weather, while another directs me to the office in the least amount of traffic. The device guides me through the entire day."

"I'm guessing that's the case for most people," Michelle added. "While access to information and helpful technology is great, the vast amounts of information available is consuming an enormous amount of our time. More importantly, it's consuming an enormous amount of our attention. With so many options from entertainment to education, we have a responsibility to consciously think about what information we should consume and not consume. We could fill an entire day just jumping from content to content. So, there are two things I suggest you do."

Michelle grabbed the pad of sticky notes, wrote on it, peeled it off, and added it to the sheet in the notebook:

Search out
positive content
for encouragement

"The first thing you need to do is search out positive content for encouragement. Some of the content we have at our fingertips is valuable, and some of it is an enormous waste of time. The content we choose to consume matters. It's vital to our personal and professional development. If you want to help overcome the negativity around you, be intentional about taking in positive messaging."

"What do you suggest?" Seth asked.

"Read inspirational books when you have time to read. Listen to positive podcasts when you're working out. Select positive music and listen to it on your commute to work. The world likely won't place positive messaging in front of you. You must be intentional about searching it out."

Michelle grabbed the pad of sticky notes, wrote the next behavior on it, peeled it off, and added it to the sheet in the notebook:

Disconnect from negative content

"The second thing you need to do is disconnect from negative content. While you are intentional about consuming positive messaging, you must be intentional about not consuming negative information."

Seth agreed. "The primary source of negative content in my life is the news. I read somewhere that 90 percent of the news is negative."

"That's probably accurate," Aaron replied with a nod, "and understandably so. I'm sure news outlets know the negativity bias in most humans will have them pay more attention to negative information than positive information. Hence, they give it to us."

"That's right. We can limit the impact of negative information by limiting what we consume. We should limit the amount of time we spend taking in the news or listening to talk radio. We should limit the amount of time we spend scrolling through social media. Consider the lyrics of the music you choose because music influences emotions. While the adage of 'Garbage In, Garbage Out' may have been intended for software development, it is equally relevant to personal growth. Be intentional about the information you let in."

"Good advice," Seth replied. "What's next?"

Proactively Reframe the Bad Stuff

"The fourth lesson is this --- proactively reframe the bad stuff. The range of challenges we face in our life is broad. From losing a loved one to breaking a nail, and from losing a job to dropping a phone. While it may all seem to be bad, we have to figure out if it is."

"Everything on that list sounds bad," Aaron replied.

"It may sound bad, but while we all experience bad stuff, we all seem to be affected differently. One person loses a best friend and says he's happy his friend is in a better place. Another person breaks a nail and reacts as if the world is coming to an end. Why is that?"

Aaron and Seth thought about it for a moment. Seth responded by saying, "Perspective."

"Perspective is certainly one answer. Another is a little more complicated. None of the bad stuff that happens to us has inherent meaning. We assign the bad stuff meaning based on how we interpret it. In other words, if we see a lost job as the loss of income and prestige, we'll assign the situation as bad. If we see a lost job as an opportunity to find a new job doing something we love, we'll assign the situation as good."

"That makes sense," Aaron replied.

"The experiences in our life are just experiences. While some are worse than others, they still are just experiences. Even when something horrific happens in your life, it is only horrific because of the way you see it. Whatever you see as awful and unbearable is nothing until you label it awful and unbearable."

Seth chimed in. "Tragedy in any form is sad. When those things that are seemingly bad occur, we need to mourn. We need to experience normal human emotions. We all will frame it as the tragedy it is."

"You are correct. Once we've experienced those normal human emotions, we can step back to look at it in the bigger picture of life. If we can frame an experience in our life based on the meaning we give it, we can reframe it once we process the tragedy. If we frame the loss of a loved one as tragic as we mourn, we can reframe it as comforting as we consider our loved one is no longer in pain. If we frame the loss of a job as devastating because we lost income, we can reframe it as positive as we consider the opportunity to learn a new skill."

"If that is true," Seth replied, "we should be able to reframe any thought in our head to something more positive. It's all about reframing --- giving positive meaning to the bad stuff. Ultimately, it allows us to gain control of how the situation is impacting us."

"Exactly, Seth. Reframing is a choice, and it's not always easy. While wallowing around in the crud is much easier, reframing will change your state of mind and get you moving again. There are two things I suggest you do."

Michelle grabbed the pad of sticky notes, wrote on it, peeled it off, and added it to the sheet in the notebook:

"The first thing you need to do is say 'good' to the bad. If any situation in our life is bad because we've labeled it bad, then we can begin to see it as good by calling it good. You got furloughed from your job for six months. Good --- you just found the time to learn a new skill. There's an accident on the highway that will make you late to work. Good --- you just found some time to listen to that positive podcast you downloaded. Your boyfriend just left you. Good --- now you can take some time to find someone who values you and treats you with respect. It's all about reframing."

"I like it," Seth replied.

Michelle grabbed the pad of sticky notes, wrote on it, peeled it off, and added it to the sheet in the notebook:

"The second thing you need to do is ask 'reframing' questions. We need to reframe things because of the way we initially framed them. Again, if we see something as bad, it's because we initially framed it as bad. One way to make reframing easier is to ask new questions. Will this situation mean anything to me in five years? Is there a lesson in this that will make me better in the future? Does this situation really make me unhappy? The answers to questions like these may make it easier to see the good in the bad."

Aaron thought about it for a moment. "As I think back on the old me, reframing the bad stuff is exactly what I always did. I just never had a name for it. I would observe a negative thought and simply replace it with a positive one. It was a choice I made back then, and one I need to start making again. What's next?"

Look for the Good Stuff

"The fifth lesson is this --- look for the good stuff. One of the reasons some people feel overwhelmed by negativity is they don't spend enough time appreciating the good stuff in their life. Since research shows that 80 percent of our daily thoughts are negative, true appreciation for the blessings in our life isn't getting much of our attention."

Aaron thought for a moment. "If I'm honest with myself, I haven't done an outstanding job of looking for the good stuff lately. I've been so busy wallowing around in my crud that I haven't lifted my head enough to see all the good stuff around me."

"One reason we don't reflect on the good is we don't consider things as being 'good' for very long," Michelle continued. "We wanted the latest and greatest cell phone when it first came out. We got it, and we were happy and appreciated it --- for a short time. We then adjusted our expectation to the new status quo and now need more, like the next upgraded cell phone, to maintain the same level of happiness."

"Why is that?" Seth asked.

"Research shows why happiness and appreciation don't last all that long. Two positive psychologists, Philip Brickman and Donald Campbell, wrote about hedonic adaptation, also referred to as the hedonic treadmill, back in 1971. The idea is that our level of happiness tends to return to where it started after the positive experience fades away. It is our happiness resting point, the place we return after good and bad experiences. It looks like this."

Michelle tore a sheet of paper from her notebook and drew a diagram:

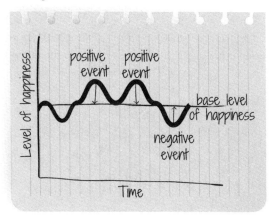

"So, we come down off of the 'high' of a positive experience?" Seth asked.

"Yes. For example, while we may have appreciated the new cell phone when we bought it, the euphoria we experienced faded quickly. We then went back to our base level of happiness. Most people think they would be elated if they won a multi-million-dollar lottery, and no doubt they would --- for a short time. Hedonic adaptation shows that the highest highs and the lowest lows fade in time. No matter how good or bad an experience makes you feel, you'll eventually return to your base level of happiness."

"I experience that all the time," Aaron added.

"Although we all return to our base level of happiness, we spend more time thinking back on the negative events because of our negativity bias. To overcome negativity in our lives, we must make an intentional effort to look for the good stuff to appreciate it. Two things I suggest you do."

Michelle grabbed the pad of sticky notes, wrote on it, peeled it off, and added it to the sheet in the notebook:

Stop comparing yourself to others

"The first thing you need to do is stop comparing yourself to others. It's hard to appreciate what we have if we constantly compare ourselves to others. No matter how much success we achieve, there will always be someone who has something we don't. We'll see someone with a better relationship, better health, and more stuff. When we compare ourselves to others, we are focusing on their blessings and ignoring our own."

"While I enjoy social media as much as anyone," Aaron admitted, "I almost always feel inadequate. I scroll through feeds where friends often showcase only the best aspects of their life. I bet it takes most people a dozen poses before they get that 'perfect' profile picture."

Seth added as he pointed at Aaron's phone. "Just like you'll pick the best shot you got of this view earlier. Probably crop and filter it before it ever makes it to social media."

Michelle nodded in agreement. "Exactly. This perfection is an illusion, and it leads to feelings of disappointment. It's hard to appreciate what we have when we feel inadequate because we've been comparing ourselves to others."

"I couldn't agree more," Seth responded. "What's next?"

Michelle grabbed the pad of sticky notes, wrote on it, peeled it off, and added it to the sheet in the notebook:

Count your collective blessings

"The next thing you need to do is count your collective blessings. It's easy to take things for granted when something goes from a desire to a perceived need in a short period. It's also easy to take things for granted when we're laser-focused on the next faster, bigger, or stronger object. At some point, we need to look around to count our collective blessings --- things other people dream about having."

"It's embarrassing how many good things we take for granted," Aaron admitted reluctantly.

"And it's not just the big things," Michelle added. "If you have access to safe drinking water, you have a blessing 780 million people in the world don't have. If you have access to proper and regular food, you have a blessing 795 million people in the world don't have. Look around --- the good stuff surrounds us."

Seth strongly agreed. "We need to practice gratitude by taking the time to count our collective blessings."

"Amen," Aaron responded. "What's next?"

Enhance the Conversation

"The sixth and final lesson is this --- enhance the conversation. Every day we encounter friends, family, colleagues, and strangers. As a habit, and as a form of good etiquette, we have a verbal greeting. Not only is it the polite thing to do, it is also basic to advanced interaction."

"Yep," Seth responded, "and the most common greeting is, 'How are you doing?' The most common response is, 'Fine, how are you?' I suppose it's a social game we play to get along with others."

"It is, and there is a problem with this simple greeting. Some people don't realize it's simply a greeting, similar to 'Good morning' or 'Hello neighbor.' They think they're supposed to respond with how they're really doing! The greeting 'How are you doing?' was never intended to be an actual question during a greeting. Sure, it's an important question when you see someone you believe is struggling with something, and they may need a friend. However, when it comes to this greeting, the proper response is to be friendly and play the game by saying, 'Fine, how are you?'"

"And there's a second problem with 'How are you doing?'" Seth added. "The greeting provides a stage for every would-be comedian who uses it as an opportunity to be witty. Ask them how they're doing, and they'll reply with, 'I'd complain, but nobody would listen,' or 'My lawyer said I didn't have to answer that question,' or 'I was fine until you asked.'"

"Or, 'I've got this strange itch on my right butt cheek'," Aaron laughed hysterically.

Seth and Michelle just stared at Aaron. Michelle continued when Aaron stopped laughing at his humor. "There's a good chance this typical greeting could turn into a conversation filled with negativity since we seem to complain at least once every minute. We need to find ways to enhance the conversation, and there are two things I suggest you do."

Michelle again grabbed the pad of sticky notes, wrote on it, peeled it off, and added it to the sheet in the notebook:

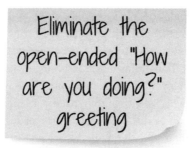

Eliminate the open-ended "How are you doing?" greeting

"The first thing you need to do is eliminate the open-ended 'How are you doing?' greeting. While it may be a standard greeting, a real and meaningful conversation will never come from you asking someone how they're doing. The chances are high that you don't want to know, and the person you're asking may want to tell you exactly how they're doing. It is a meaningless exchange."

"Agreed," Seth replied.

Michelle continued. "Since this ritualized greeting allows for way too much negativity for those who don't realize it's just a greeting, eliminate 'How are you doing?' from your greeting. That's right, unless you really want to know how someone is doing, don't ask the question. Instead, replace it with a challenge."

Michelle grabbed the pad of sticky notes, wrote on it, peeled it off, and added it to the sheet in the notebook:

Transition to the "Tell Me Somethin' Good!" greeting

"The second thing you need to do is transition to the *'Tell Me Somethin' Good!'* greeting. If you eliminate 'How are you doing?' from your greeting, you need to replace it with something meaningful. You need to replace it with something that will enhance the conversation ---

something that will encourage others to find the good in their life. Replace it with this one simple phrase, 'Tell Me Somethin' Good!'"

Aaron thought about it for a moment. "That's how you greeted Seth in the bar earlier this evening. I was hoping you wouldn't turn to me and ask the same question, but now I get it. This is more than a greeting --- this is a challenge. People can't share something negative when you ask them to share something good. 'Tell Me Somethin' Good!' forces them to consider something positive. I love it!"

"You will be amazed how this one simple phrase can completely enhance the conversation. The opportunity for mind-numbing negativity that comes from the open-ended greeting of 'How are you doing?' is gone. As you said, a personal challenge for someone to search for something good in life to share has replaced it."

"It seems a key to overcoming negativity is to get people focused on the good stuff in their life," Aaron added. "The current way of greeting others by asking how they are doing is setting us up for conversational failure. Asking someone to tell us something good in their life is enhancing the conversation, one challenge at a time."

"Of everything you've shared," Seth replied, "that may be the easiest to implement. What's next?"

"That's it," Michelle answered. "Six lessons with twelve behaviors. None of it is hard. Like anything, the application of the ideas will determine the effectiveness. The only way any of us can overcome the negativity in our lives is to implement the ideas."

Aaron sat quietly for a moment. "You're right, Michelle. You didn't mention a single thing I'm not capable of doing. It's just a matter of whether or not I'm committed to improving. I can't tell you how much I appreciate you taking the time to share your thoughts. You did your part by sharing the advice, and now it's time for me to do my part by applying it to my life. I promise you I'll do it. Let's call it a night. We have a full day at the conference tomorrow."

The three of them shook hands and headed back into the hotel. Not long after Aaron got to his room, he received an e-mail from Michelle with the PDF summary and the link to the 30-Day Challenge she had promised. Michelle had kept her promise --- now it was time for Aaron to keep his.

Conclusion

The lessons taught in this book are simple. I suppose I could have written it in a complicated, scientific way to make it look more difficult, but what's the point. We already make life more complicated than it needs to be. We need more simple solutions.

I spoke in Minnesota years ago and encountered an older gentleman at the end of my speech. He asked, "Where is the new stuff? Everything I heard you say today I've heard in some form throughout my life. I want some new stuff!"

I looked at him for a moment and said, "I'll give you the new stuff as soon as you get the old stuff right." Like this man in Minnesota, we're in constant search of new stuff while we step right over the meaningful, simple things that we already know will make us better.

This book contains many of the meaningful, simple things that can help you overcome negativity.

Simple things that will enhance the lives of people around you when you help them overcome their negativity. Simple things that will improve your own experience when you help yourself overcome your negativity.

We need more simple solutions. It is my hope you embrace the simple solutions in this book to enhance your life.

Acknowledgments

To those who have helped share the *Tell Me Somethin' Good!* challenge over the past 20 years.

To those who naturally lean toward the good stuff in life. You are an inspiration to others.

To those who want to be more positive and just need to change behavior.

To Christa Geraghty and Barbie Todd for making the manuscript better.

To Billy Long for the generous donation to the First Chance Foundation in return for having Michelle Chase's name appear in the fable.

To my family and friends for being a part of my journey, and letting me be part of yours.

To God, the Creator of all that is good. Thank you for allowing it all to happen.

About the Author

Clint is the president and CEO of Verbalocity, Inc., a personal development company with a focus on leadership enhancement. For the past two decades, he has worked to enhance corporate culture as a speaker, trainer, consultant, and coach.

He has traveled the world working with Fortune 500 companies, government agencies, and trade associations. He has delivered his programs throughout the United States, Canada, South America, the United Kingdom, Central America, Mexico, Bermuda, and the Bahamas.

Clint is the author of *Engaged Leadership: Building a Culture to Overcome Employee Disengagement* (Wiley, 2007 and 2011) and *Living for the Weekday: What Every Employee and Boss Needs to Know about Enjoying Work and Life* (Wiley, 2010).

Clint lives with his wife Heather of 18 years in Bulverde, Texas, just north of San Antonio in the Texas Hill Country where they have raised their five girls (Black, Bleu, Bailey, Bacon, and Banjo --- their five dogs)!

To learn more about Clint and Verbalocity, visit www. verbalocity.com.

Next Steps

Here are the next steps to help you build a positive culture using the *Tell Me Somethin' Good!* message:

(1) Download the free 30-Day Challenge. You can find it at www.findthegoodinlife.com.

(2) Give a copy of the *Tell Me Somethin' Good!* book to every employee in your office, and encourage them all to take the 30-Day Challenge together.

(3) Go even further and put a *Tell Me Somethin' Good!* Boost Box on every employee's desk to reinforce the message on a daily basis. You can find the Boost Box at www.findthegoodinlife.com.

(4) Make *Tell Me Somethin' Good!* a theme for your company or department to embrace all year.

(5) Form a *Tell Me Somethin' Good!* private group on social media to regularly share the good stuff.

(6) Give a copy of *Tell Me Somethin' Good!* to friends and family to spread the good stuff.

(7) Produce a private-label print version of *Tell Me Somethin' Good!* with a personalized note from you as the forward to the book.

(8) Offer the *Tell Me Somethin' Good!* book or Boost Box as a meeting or convention gift for all attendees to reinforce your theme.

(9) Download and subscribe to the *Tell Me Somethin' Good!* podcast with Clint Swindall.